Mystery Shopping Empire

Creating a Successful Secret Shopping Business

Table of Contents

Chapter 1. Introduction

Unearth the secrets of a thriving and rewarding commercial world with our Special Report: "Mystery Shopping Empire: Creating a Successful Secret Shopping Business." Packed with detailed, step-by-step instructions, engaging insights, and business tips from industry experts, this report offers you the key to unlock an entirely new realm of opportunities. Are you ready to step into a life of intriguing assignments, flexible schedules, and substantial income? Prepare yourself to become the mastermind of your very own successful mystery shopping venture. With our Special Report, not only will you set your foot into this fascinating field, but you'll also master the art of creating, managing, and flourishing a secret shopping entity, all from the comfort of your home, on your terms. So, why wait? Embrace the mystery, seize the opportunity, and transform your financial future today!

Chapter 2. Unlocking the World of Mystery Shopping

Mystery shopping is an intriguing and rewarding field that provides businesses with valuable insights about their customer service, the effectiveness of their employee training programs, and their product quality, among other things. But it also offers aspiring entrepreneurs unique opportunities to create and manage their own flourishing enterprises. Let's delve deeper into what this world looks like and how one can succeed in it.

2.1. Understanding Mystery Shopping

Mystery shopping, sometimes also referred to as secret shopping, involves individuals who pose as regular customers to monitor and measure service quality. The mystery shopper typically performs specific tasks such as purchasing a product, asking questions, or behaving in a certain way, and then provides detailed reports or feedback on their experience.

Businesses hire mystery shopping services for a variety of reasons. They might be interested in understanding how their employees interact with customers, how effectively their products are sold, or even to keep an eye on their competition. As a mystery shopping service owner, you will be responsible for providing individuals - your shoppers - who can go undercover and gather this data for them.

2.2. Starting Your Mystery Shopping Business

Starting a mystery shopping business doesn't require a significant financial investment. The following are key steps in setting up your business.

1. Register your business: Provide it with a legal structure by deciding whether it will be a sole proprietorship, a partnership, a limited liability company, or a corporation.

2. Create a business plan: Define your goals, target market, operational structure, and financial forecasts.

3. Establish a website: This will serve as your virtual business card, giving potential clients information about your services. Ensure your website is easy to navigate and aesthetically pleasing, with all relevant information easily accessible.

4. Hire shoppers: Look for reliable, articulate individuals who are good at remembering details.

2.3. Creating Effective Mystery Shopping Assignments

A well-executed mystery shopping assignment provides valuable insights. Some factors to consider in creating effective assignments are:

1. Being specific about what data to collect: Instead of statements like "Observe staff friendliness," opt for clear, measurable instructions, such as "Note if a staff member greets you within five minutes of entering."

2. Providing detailed guidelines: The more specific the instructions, the more useful the feedback.

3. Creating real-life scenarios: This helps in capturing authentic responses from the business being evaluated.

4. Ensuring anonymity: The shopper's anonymity should be preserved, as any slip can affect the genuineness of the experience.

2.4. Managing Your Business Effectively

Once your business is operational, how you manage it will determine its success. Important factors to consider include:

1. Building strong relationships with clients and shoppers: Maintaining regular communication and seeing to their needs can foster loyalty and create a sustainable client base.

2. Monitoring assignments: Conduct regular checks to ensure that assignments are being carried out to the standards of your company. This may involve follow-up calls and feedback sessions.

3. Offering competitive pricing: Set your fees based on what your target market is willing to pay, and consider what your competition is charging.

4. Upgrading your skills: Regularly attending workshops and seminars on customer service and mystery shopping can help you stay updated and allow you to offer better services.

Mystery shopping is a fascinating field that requires diligence, attention to detail, and the ability to understand and meet clients' needs. As an entrepreneur in this field, you have the opportunity to create a business that not only provides a valuable service but also offers flexibility, constant learning, and the satisfaction of contributing to the enhancement of customer service across various industries. The key is to stay focused, committed, and always be on the lookout for ways to improve and grow.

Chapter 3. Essential Skills for a Successful Mystery Shopper

Being a successful mystery shopper requires an array of essential skills. While the role might appear straightforward on the surface, a deeper understanding of divergent factors — from psychology to operational dynamics, and from report writing to scheduling — is necessary to excel. Whether you perceive mystery shopping as a part-time income source or aim to build a full-fledged business around it, the crux of the job consists of adopting various skills that differentiate a good mystery shopper from a great one.

3.1. Observational Skills

As a mystery shopper, your vision is your primary tool. You need to observe and document everything around you without seeming out of place. This means watching for details about cleanliness, employee behaviors, promotional materials, and even customer reactions. Your work effectively creates an evidential record of the business you are assigned to review.

When professionally observing, remember not to rely solely on your memory. After each task, make it a habit to jot down pertinent details, pay attention to nuances, and capture the essence of the environment. Attach photos, if possible, as they provide additional support to your observations.

3.2. Communication Skills

Mystery shoppers are communicators at heart. Often, you'll find yourself in situations where you need to engage with staff without revealing your true motive. Thus, you need superior verbal and non-verbal communication skills.

It's not just about asking questions; it's about asking the right questions. Being able to lead a conversation subtly in a direction that will yield the information you need is an art. Additionally, your body language should blend with the environment, convincing the staff that you are just another customer.

And it doesn't stop at verbal exchanges. The true test of your communication skills is when you translate your observations into concise, clear, and professional reports to your clients. Wordsmithing is crucial in this job; your reports should be comprehensive, well-articulated, typo-free, and reader-friendly.

3.3. Analytical Skills

The ability to interpret and analyze your observations critically is a vital part of your job. But what does analytical thinking mean in the context of mystery shopping?

Realistically, businesses hire mystery shoppers to identify gaps in their customer service, after all, that's how they improve. Thus, your role extends beyond merely observing; it involves analyzing situations, identifying improvement areas, and recommending possible solutions. You don't just report facts, you interpret them, analyze the service user's experience, and offer insights that can help the businesses refine their operations.

3.4. Scheduling and Timeliness

In the world of mystery shopping, deadlines are sacrosanct. The companies you work for depend on the timely delivery of your reports to make essential business decisions. They expect findings to be shared at the earliest so they can implement necessary changes.

Moreover, as a mystery shopper, you may be handling multiple assignments at a time. Here, your scheduling skills come to the fore.

Prioritizing tasks based on their urgency, scheduling visits, and delivering reports on time — these are all part and parcel of the job that entail a well-structured plan and time management.

3.5. Ethics and Honesty

Above any skill, the profession calls for high ethical standards. By becoming a mystery shopper, you enter a trust-based contract with your employer. They trust you with their brand reputation, customer data, and operational secrets. Any form of dishonesty or unethical behavior can not only result in immediate termination but also tarnish your reputation in the industry.

So, be brutally honest with your reviews. Sugarcoating or exaggerating realities will eventually harm the company you're reviewing and your credibility as a mystery shopper.

3.6. Patience and Persistence

Mystery shopping is not always glamorous. There will be days filled with mundane tasks, strict deadlines, and frustrating experiences. Patience and persistence will see you through these challenging times. Allegiance to the job is critical, especially when job satisfaction seems remote.

Remember, your persistence goes beyond completing a task. At times, you might have to visit a place several times before you can gather substantial information, or, you might need to wait extensively to test a particular aspect of customer service.

3.7. Adapting On-the-Fly

Mystery shopping is the world of unscripted interactions. To be successful in your job, you must become adept at adapting on-the-fly to changing situations. This might mean posing as a disinterested customer, an unhappy customer, or even a shoplifter, depending upon the assignment. Being able to modify your behavior spontaneously while retaining your cover is an essential part of the job.

Balancing all these skills isn't easy, but with practice and perseverance, they synergize to create a successful mystery shopper who adds value to businesses and bolsters customer experiences. After all, you're not just a secret shopper; you're part of an invisible force that keeps the wheels of the commercial world turning.

Chapter 4. Building Your Secret Shopper Brand

Just as with any successful business, creating your mystery shopping brand requires careful consideration, strategic planning, and creative efforts. Your brand isn't just your name, logo, or tagline. It's essentially the image your business projects and how you want customers to perceive your service. As the face of your venture, your brand should evoke trust, reliability and professionalism. Below, we will delve into this exciting journey of building your secret shopper brand.

4.1. Understanding the Importance of a Brand

A strong brand will not only help distinguish you from competitors but also develop a sense of credibility and reliability amongst clients and shoppers. It's the foundation of your business identity, setting the tone for your marketing activities and business relationships. Understanding this critical role of branding, you should invest time and resources into creating a brand that resonates with your business vision and target audience.

4.2. Creating a Brand Identity

Your brand identity comprises each and every element that shapes the perception of your company in the minds of the stakeholders: the clients who hire you and the secret shoppers who work for you. Two critical aspects of your identity are visual and communicative components.

The visual components include your logo, colors, typography, and overall design aesthetics. While the communicative aspect involves your brand voice, messaging, values, and brand story. How you combine these elements impacts how your brand is perceived and talked about.

Think about what you, as a mystery shopping company, represent and the characteristics you want associated with your brand. Are you reliable and thorough? Are you innovative and technology-driven? Defining these traits will help you formulate an identity that appeals to your target demographic.

4.3. Naming Your Business

Naming your business is an art unto itself. The ideal business name should be one that is catchy, easy to remember, and preferably one that encapsulates what your business is all about. Ensure your business name isn't too similar to another existing business, particularly within the same industry. Run thorough checks; consider an online domain name and social media handle availability as well.

4.4. Designing the Perfect Logo

Your logo is one of the first things a customer will notice about your brand. Therefore, it needs to include elements that resonate with your brand's values and stand out in the highly competitive mystery shopping industry.

Remember: simplicity is key. A clean, uncluttered logo is often more successful than a complex design. As well, choose colors that match with your brand's intended feeling. For instance, green often symbolizes freshness and growth, while blue can signify trust and calm.

When creating your logo, consider using professional help or a specialized design platform. This ensures a high-quality output that is optimized for different uses, be it for shirts, business cards or social media use.

4.5. Brand Voice and Messaging

Develop a consistent brand voice that carries throughout all your communication. This could be casual or authoritative, depending on your target audience and the image you wish to project. Your language and tone should resonate with your target audience and encourage them to trust and engage with your brand.

The same goes for your brand messaging. It's a narrative that defines your value proposition, core values and promises to your customers. It should be powerful enough to influence their perception and inspire action.

4.6. Creating a Brand Strategy

Developing an effective brand strategy begins with understanding your market and competition. Perform thorough competitive analysis to understand the strategies other mystery shopping businesses use: What seems to work? What doesn't?

Segment your target audience by defining your ideal clients and shoppers. Define their behaviors, interests, tendencies, and shopping preferences. Armed with this knowledge, optimize your branding to cater to their needs and expectations.

Finally, define clear, measurable goals for your brand, whether it's reaching a particular revenue target, partnering with certain businesses for your services, or achieving a specific customer satisfaction rating. Having these goals in mind will guide your branding efforts.

4.7. The Role of Social Media

In today's digital age, it is impossible to ignore the role of social media in brand building. Each platform allows you to refine your messaging to suit different portions of your audience and provide immediate, personalized service.

Social media is also an excellent tool for demonstrating your brand personality in a more relaxed and engaging manner. Creative posts, social engagement, and swift response to customer queries can all go a long way towards establishing a strong brand image.

With these foundational elements firmly in place, you're all set to embark on the fascinating process of transforming an exciting idea into a lucrative mystery shopping business. Remember, brand building takes time and persistence. Maintain consistency throughout each stage of your business growth and remember: the strongest brands live and breathe their values in every business aspect, from the very first client interaction to dealing with feedback and complaints.

Chapter 5. Managing Your Mystery Shopper Assignments

Time management, organizational skills, and resourcefulness form the central pivot upon which efficient mystery shopping operations revolve. As the captain of your mystery shopping enterprise, it is crucial to take a strategic approach to manage your assignments.

5.1. Understanding the Scope of the Assignment

Each mystery shopping assignment is unique and requires a distinctive approach. These can range from simple tasks like inquiring about a product's availability to complex ones like conducting a detailed on-site assessment of a business.

To manage your assignments effectively, ensure you thoroughly understand the requirements of each task. You should know the performance metrics, timelines, and the client's expected outcomes. Familiarize yourself with the detailed instructions mentioned in the assignment, and clarify any doubts before moving on to the execution phase.

5.2. Scheduling Assignments

Once you have a full grasp of the tasks ahead, it's time to schedule your assignments. With various assignments on hand, efficiently managing your schedule becomes a significant challenge.

Develop a daily, weekly, or monthly plan considering the due dates of your assignments, their complexity, and your availability. Ensure you allocate ample time for preparation, execution, and reporting. Remember, rushing through assignments can lead to missing relevant details, which diminishes the value of your service.

5.3. Gathering Necessary Tools and Resources

Proper tools and resources pave the way for smooth execution of your mystery shopping assignments. These tools could be physical assets like a camera for capturing required evidence, or digital tools like a smartphone with GPS and internet connection for navigation and instant reporting.

Identify the resources necessary for each assignment well in advance to avoid last minute rush and disappointing outcomes. Also, don't forget to maintain a proper equipment checklist for each assignment.

5.4. Executing the Assignment

Execution is where the rubber meets the road. As the mystery shopper, you ought to behave as an ordinary consumer would but remain vigilant to evaluate all aspects direct or indirect pertaining to the service.

Always adhere to the guidelines provided by your client. Incorporate fairness in your assessment and avoid personal biases. Discretion is key; your identity as a mystery shopper must remain hiddden at all times to not affect the natural course of service you are to evaluate.

5.5. Documenting the Findings

Every mystery shopping assignment concludes with documenting and submitting your findings. Consistency and precision are key here.

Organize your notes, photos, or any other pieces of evidence in the order of the assignment, ensuring it tells a logical, comprehensive story of your experience. Be clear, detailed, and objective in your reporting.

5.6. Assignment Debrief and Feedback

After submitting your findings, there's usually a debriefing session where you discuss your experiences and observations with the client. Prior to these sessions, review your reports to ensure you are familiar with every detail.

These sessions offer an opportunity to improve your service by receiving direct feedback from the client. Understand their concerns and expectations better with each post-assignment debrief and align your future operations accordingly.

Managing assignments in your mystery shopping business is a dynamic process that requires keen observation, strategic planning, and exceptional execution skills. By refining these aspects of your business, you'd not just provide tremendous value to your clients but also ensure the sustainability and growth of your mystery shopping business.

Remember that every assignment you undertake is a learning opportunity. Take the lessons from each completed assignment and use them to improve your next. The resilience and adaptability you display will reflect on the growth trajectory of your mystery shopping empire.

Chapter 6. Mastering the Art of Observation and Reporting

Observation is much more than just looking around. It's about taking in the minute details, understanding what's going on, and making connections. In the context of mystery shopping, honing your observational skills is indispensable, as it forms the backbone of successful and accurate reporting.

When embarking on a mystery shopping assignment, you need to observe, remember, and report on numerous parameters including customer service, product availability, cleanliness, and more. However, before you can master the art of observation for mystery shopping, it's essential to understand what it encompasses.

6.1. Critical Elements of Observation

Observation in mystery shopping involves both active and passive observation. Active observation refers to actively seeking information. For example, asking queries from customer service or noticing the color schemes of the product branding. Passive observation, on the other hand, is about understanding and retaining information acquired subconsciously.

Though these distinctions exist, the truth is that good observation naturally combines both. Successful mystery shoppers use a blend of active and passive observation throughout their assignments.

To start, you need a game plan. One crucial aspect of successful mystery shopping is knowing what to observe. It will be overwhelming (and pointless) to try to remember every possible detail you come across. You should have a hierarchy of observations.

6.2. Develop Your Observational Framework

The observational framework should be developed based on the requirements of the specific mystery shopping assignment. For instance, if a coffee shop has hired you, they might be interested in how quickly the service is, whether the coffee is served hot, the cleanliness of the outlet, or the behavior of the staff.

In our coffee shop case, note the following:

- Time taken from placing the order to receiving it

- The temperature of the coffee at the time of receiving

- The cleanliness of the tables, counters, and overall premises

- Any specific behavior from the staff that stood out (positive or negative)

6.3. Techniques for Enhancing Observation

Here are a few tricks to enhance your observational skills:

- Be Curiously Aware: Adopt an exploratory mindset. This means you ask questions, look for information, and are generally curious about things. This will help you notice details you would otherwise skip.

- Use All Your Senses: Good observation is not just about the eyes. It's about all senses. Is the place smelling foul? Is there a disturbing noise? Is the place too hot or too cold?

- Practice Mindfulness: This means being in the present moment. When you are mindful, you take in more information about your surroundings and are more likely to recall them later.

6.4. Sharpening Reporting Skills

Reporting is what gets you the paychecks. Every mystery shopping assignment ends with a report that covers your observations and experiences. This report will be shared with the client, and often, important business decisions will be made based on your feedback. Therefore, it is extremely crucial to get it right.

6.5. Effective Report Writing Tips

Here are some tips which can enhance your report writing skills:

- Be Specific: General observations won't be helpful for the client. Be as specific as you can. Instead of saying "The staff was nice," you can say, "The server greeted me with a warm smile and politely took my order."

- Be Honest: Your report has to be an accurate representation of your experience. It's not a critique for the sake of it. If you had a good experience, the report should reflect that.

- Stick to the Facts: Your report should be devoid of personal opinions. Keep your report purely factual and based on your observations. Avoid dramatizing.

- Clear and Concise Language: Keep the language simple and straightforward. You wouldn't want to risk confusing your client with jargon or complicated sentences.

6.6. Practicing Observation and Reporting

To truly master the observation and the art of reporting, practice is key. Put yourself in diverse shopping situations and monitor your observational skills. Try writing reports for each experience and have someone critique your work. The aim is to provide the most value to your clients in a concise, easy-to-understand, honest, and professional report.

Remember, the more attention you pay to details, the more accurate your report will be, and the more value you can offer to the assignment. And eventually, the greater the success you will achieve in your mystery shopping venture.

To conclude, the art of observation and reporting in mystery shopping is a skilled task. With proper understanding, practical implementations, and constant practice, you will surely succeed in mastering these skills. Doing so will make you an invaluable asset to your mystery shopping company and contribute significantly to its success and growth.

Chapter 7. Expanding Your Business: Opportunities and Challenges

After establishing your mystery shopping business, the next step is to think about expansion. You have laid a strong foundation, built a reputation, and now it's time to scale up. But that comes with its own set of opportunities and challenges. An understanding of these will prepare you for the journey ahead.

7.1. Identifying Expansion Opportunities

Expansion opportunities may include broadening the scope of your services, pursuing a new type of client, franchising, or establishing partnerships with other businesses. Each of these offers a unique potential for growth, but also brings different challenges and considerations.

When broadening your services, consider how your existing skills and resources can be leveraged. Does your shopper team have a unique skill set that could be utilized in additional ways? For example, if you have a team of shoppers who are particularly adept at evaluating customer service, you might expand into surveying employee performance across other domains.

Alternatively, you might pursue new types of clients, perhaps extending from retail into hospitality or finance. Each industry has its own nuances and may require different approaches, but they all share the need for feedback and customer experience improvement.

Franchising is another opportunity. It allows you to grow your business without having to manage every aspect of every location. You provide the franchisee with your business model and brand, and they manage the operations in their location.

Finally, partnerships with other businesses, particularly those within related industries, could be an excellent opportunity. For example, pairing with a consulting firm could allow you to offer a holistic solution where you provide the feedback and data, and your partner assists the client in implementing solutions.

7.2. Understanding The Challenges

While these opportunities offer great potential, they also come with challenges. Expanding the scope of services requires investment in training and potentially hiring more staff. You'll need to pitch your new services not only to new clients but also to existing ones. And, there's no guarantee these services will be as successful as your core offerings.

Moving into new industries requires getting up to speed with industry-specific protocols and procedures, which can be time-consuming. There's also increased competition as you're entering a space where other mystery shopping businesses may already be established.

Franchising introduces an element of control loss. You're trusting someone else to run a business under your brand. It requires careful selection of franchise partners and in-depth training to ensure they preserve the quality and reputation of your brand.

Creating partnerships is not just about signing an agreement. Collaborations may fail due to mismatched expectations or miscommunication. Clear, consistent communication and well-defined roles and responsibilities are essential for the success of partnerships.

7.3. Developing a Strategic Expansion Plan

A strategic expansion plan will be your guide through this phase. It should outline the why, what, when, where, and how of your planned expansion. Identify your expansion goals and consider the opportunities we've discussed. Decide which fit best with your business's vision and capabilities.

A thorough SWOT (Strengths, Weaknesses, Opportunities, Threats) analysis can offer some beneficial insights. This strategic planning technique allows you to understand your internal and external environment better, and to make more informed decisions.

7.4. Managing Change in Your Business

Introducing changes in your business comes with its own set of challenges. People are naturally resistant to change and might fear their jobs being at risk, or worry about how changes might affect their roles. It's crucial to manage change appropriately to prevent such issues from arising.

Firstly, communicate clearly and frequently. Employees should be aware of the changes, why they're happening, and how they'll be impacted. Address any concerns promptly and honestly. Then, involve your staff in the change process to increase buy1in. Providing training and support will also help smooth the transition.

7.5. Managing Business Finances during Expansion

Expansion often requires a significant financial outlay. You may need to invest in additional staff, training, equipment, or locations. It's essential to have a detailed financial plan accounting for all possible expenditures, alongside projected earnings.

Also, consider the financial risks. Expansion may not be as profitable as you hope, especially in the early days. It's important to have a plan in place to manage any potential financial shortfall.

As you expand your mystery shopping business, you open up new possibilities for growth and success. With careful planning, a clear vision, and a strong strategy, you can overcome the challenges and seize the opportunities expansion offers.

Chapter 8. Financial Aspects: Pricing, Negotiation, and Profitability

Formulating a precise, profitable pricing strategy, equipping oneself with negotiation skills, and understanding, anticipating, and optimizing profitability are critical components of any successful business venture, including a mystery shopping enterprise. Accurate financial management can boost your business, ensuring a consistent cash flow and paving the way for a stable, lucrative future.

8.1. Pricing Your Services

The heart of your mystery shopping business is your service offering. Establishing a pricing model is critical. Incorrect pricing can negatively impact your profitability and even lead your business into insolvency.

To begin with, conduct a comprehensive market analysis, studying your competitors, their pricing models, and value offerings. Understanding the ongoing rates in your geographical and operational area can give you a benchmark to start.

Also, consider the costs associated with each assignment. Working costs can include transport, meals, or purchases required during the shopping experience, while administrative overheads include utilities, software, or hiring personnel.

Here's a standard template to calculate your service price:

```
Assignment costs (direct expenses) + Overhead costs
(indirect expenses) + Desired Profit Margin (%) =
```

Remember that your pricing should not only cover your costs but should also allow you to make a profit after all expenses.

8.2. Negotiation Skills

Dealing with clients and service providers requires a level of negotiation skill to come to mutually agreeable terms. A mystery shopping business entails negotiating contract terms, prices, and timelines, among others.

Developing these soft skills is critical in establishing your business. Consider undertaking negotiation training, either through books, online courses, or mentorships.

Remember, effective negotiation is never about winning or losing but reaching a solution that benefits both parties. Don't be hesitant to walk away from a deal that doesn't resonate with your business model or ethics.

8.3. Profitability

Profit is the ultimate goal when starting and growing a business. For mystery shopping businesses, profitability stems from:

- Regular flow of assignments
- Controlled Costs
- Competitive and profitable pricing
- Effective negotiations
- Adequate utilization of resources

Monitoring and boosting profitability requires vigilant financial management. A balanced scorecard approach can be beneficial in gauging your business's financial health:

1. Financial Perspective: Revenue, Profits, Return On Investment (ROI)

2. Customer Perspective: Customer Satisfaction, Retention Rate

3. Internal Processes Perspective: Efficiency of Processes, Cost Management

4. Learning & Growth Perspective: Employee Satisfaction, Skills Enhancement

Regularly use this scorecard to do a SWOT Analysis (Strengths, Weaknesses, Opportunities, Threats) of your business.

Finally, always keep an eye on your overheads (the ongoing business expenses not directly attributed to creating a product or service). Keeping overheads under control can drastically impact profitability. This can be achieved by working remotely, utilizing technology, and outsourcing non-core tasks.

8.4. Conclusion

Understanding the financial aspects of your mystery shopping business can act as a catalyst for your growth and success. Pricing your services appropriately ensures you remain competitive while covering costs and securing profit. Negotiating confidently ensures good business relationships, and focusing on profitability helps in financial planning and stability. By mastering these aspects, you can secure a solid financial future for your business. By building on your financial acumen, you can transform your business into a substantial and rewarding mystery shopping empire.

Chapter 9. Bridging the Gap: Communications and Relationships with Clients

Mastering the art of communication and relationship building with your clients lies at the core of building a successful mystery shopping empire. It revolves around understanding their needs and expectations, and delivering beyond those parameters.

9.1. The Power of Effective Communication

Communication is the key to successful business interactions. Your ability to articulate your services, understand client expectations, and follow through on those expectations is essential for building a strong client relationship.

When it comes to mystery shopping, the communication model becomes more complex due to the secret nature of your business. You may be interacting with a business owner one day, and their frontline employee the next — and your style and technique of communication for each of these individuals should differ considerably. This is where your adaptive communication skills are put to the test.

9.2. Building Strong Foundations

Just like any relationship, consistency is key. Delivering what you promise consistently will build a strong foundation for your relationship with your clients.

Consider these simple yet important steps: 1. Understand the client's needs – Invest time in understanding your client's business model, culture, and specific needs. Function as a business consultant rather than a service provider. 2. Establish clear expectations - Clearly outline what the client should expect from your services, including objective measurements, timeframes, and deliverables. 3. Deliver on your commitments – Nothing breaks trust faster than broken promises. Ensure that you are able to deliver on the expectations you've set out.

9.3. Adaptability: Changing Comms to Suit Client Types

Understanding a client's personality and adapting your communication style to suit them is one of the most effective ways to build a strong relationship. Some clients may prefer straight-to-the-point communication, while others may appreciate a more detailed approach. Being versatile in your communication style will lead to more positive outcomes and long-lasting relationships.

9.4. The Art of Receiving Feedback

Being open to feedback from your clients is crucial. Adopt a habit of seeking feedback, whether it's positive or constructive. This shows your clients that you value their input and are committed to improving your services. But, receiving feedback is only the first step. It's crucial how you respond to it and implement changes.

9.5. Nurturing Client Relationships

Building a relationship doesn't end when a project concludes. It's all about nurturing a rapport that encourages repeat business and referrals. This can be achieved through follow-ups, staying in touch via newsletters, or addressing concerns promptly.

In time, and with diligent nurturing, you'll find that your clients begin to value not just your services, but also the relationship you've built with them. This will drive longevity and success for your mystery shopping venture.

In conclusion, remember that good communication and strong relationships with clients are the bedrock of a successful mystery shopping business. Building these skills takes time and patience, but the rewards are valuable and long-lasting.

Chapter 10. Coping with Unexpected Scenarios: Tips and Tricks

As a mystery shopper, you will more often than not find yourself in situations that deviate from the normal script. Depending on the assignment, these deviations might include an employee going off-script or unexpected incidents happening at the location that impact your ability to fulfill your assignment. Here are some advice and strategies to help you navigate these scenarios effectively.

10.1. Navigating Employee Suspicion

When on assignment, maintaining your undercover status is paramount. But sometimes, you may encounter employees who are suspicious of your activities. In such cases, how do you handle the situation?

Firstly, always remain calm. Displaying nervousness will only serve to confirm their suspicion. Remember, you're doing nothing wrong – you're only performing a customer service evaluation.

Then, deflect any direct questions about being a mystery shopper with a question of your own. For instance, if an employee asks, "Are you a mystery shopper?", you could respond with, "What is a mystery shopper?" This won't arouse suspicions as most people have likely never heard of a mystery shopper.

10.2. Handling Unforeseen Circumstances

Unforeseen circumstances can range from natural disasters like flooding to human-induced events such as a fire alarm going off, forcing the shutdown of the location you're evaluating. If such a thing happens while you're on assignment, safety must be your number one priority. Once you're safe, let your mystery shopping company know about the situation as soon as possible. They will guide you on the next steps and how to proceed with the project, if possible.

10.3. Dealing with Negative Experiences

During your assignments, there may be times when you encounter negative customer service experiences. It's vital to remember that your role is, above all, to objectively report what happens. Furthermore, don't forget to document everything: the good, the bad, and the neutral. Always provide objective feedback, backed by facts, not personal feelings or opinions.

Even when you encounter something very unpleasant or unethical, you must maintain your disguise. Don't reveal your identity to try and 'correct' the situation. Report to your mystery shopping company, and they will handle the situation.

10.4. Managing Personal Interactions

At times, an assignment may require you to interact with an employee or another customer. Here, you have to balance between maintaining your secret shopper identity and ensuring your interaction doesn't come off as forced or abnormal.

If you're asked personal questions that could expose your assignment, weave a believable story that deflects attention from your mystery shopping task. Remember, your goal is to blend in with the average customer, so avoid overly elaborate stories.

10.5. Dealing with Failures

In some situations, despite your best efforts, an assignment might not go as planned. Perhaps you forgot to ask a critical question, missed an important observation, or couldn't complete all tasks due to an unexpected interruption.

When faced with such a scenario, don't panic. Reach out to your mystery shopping company and explain the situation. They can provide guidance on whether you should return to complete the assignment or if the done parts will be sufficient. Remember, mistakes are part of the learning process, so don't be too hard on yourself.

10.6. The Awe of Authenticity

To create an authentic experience and keep your cover intact, do a dry run of the shopping scenario wherever possible. This helps in predicting possible challenges and preparing for them, making your responses seem natural and spontaneous. It's also helpful to dress appropriately for the scenario and avoid taking too many notes publicly, which might give you away.

Remember, the key is not to attract special attention. You want to blend into the typical customer profile as much as possible so that your observations and interviews will be valid.

Ensuring consistency throughout these unexpected scenarios is one of the critical aspects of being a successful mystery shopper. Patience, commitment, and flexibility are equally essential traits. With practice, these situations will become less intimidating and more manageable. Remember, each assignment is a unique experience, providing a chance to enhance your skills and drive your mystery shopping business to success. Keep pushing forward, learning from and adapting to each situation you encounter.

Chapter 11. Evolving in the Empire: Growth and Sustainability Strategies

Today, let's dive into a world where growth and sustainability intertwine, where planning meets execution to yield incredible results. The journey we undertake today will involve the expansion and long-term sustenance of your newly established mystery shopping venture.

11.1. Understanding Your Business Environment

The first step towards growth involves understanding the business environment you operate in. A comprehensive analysis of both internal and external industry factors is crucial. Start by identifying your strengths, weaknesses, opportunities, and threats (SWOT). Your strengths and weaknesses are internal – aspects of your operations you can directly control. Opportunities and threats, on the other hand, are external – they arise from the market or industry.

For example, a strength could be your extensive network of mystery shoppers, a weakness could be a lack of experience, opportunities could include a market with few competitors, and threats could be changes in consumer legislation. By understanding these elements, you'll be better equipped to create strategies to leverage your strengths and opportunities, mitigate your weaknesses, and neutralize threats.

11.2. Building Scalable Systems

Scalability is key for any growth-oriented venture. As your business expands, you will need systems that can handle increased demand without faltering. From recruitment processes to databases to shopper payment procedures, all these systems need to be scalable. Begin by identifying potential stress points in your current systems and brainstorm solutions. An example might be updating your older data system with a cloud-based system that grows as you do.

11.3. Bolstering Your Shopper Network

A reliable and extensive network of mystery shoppers is a crucial asset for your business. You'll need shoppers who are dependable, observant, and disciplined. Consider creating a thorough and effective recruitment process. For retaining shoppers, regularly recognize and reward their work. Training programs can also ensure shoppers deliver consistent and high-quality work.

11.4. Offering Excellent Client Service

Retention of existing clients is just as crucial as acquiring new ones. Clients will stick with your business if they consistently receive excellent service that exceeds their expectations. Regular communication, prompt responsiveness to inquiries, and delivering high-quality reports are ways to ensure your clients are satisfied.

11.5. Diversifying Your Portfolio

As your business expands, diversify your client portfolio across different sectors. This spreads risk and opens up new opportunities. No industry is off-limits for a mystery shopping business — from retail to hospitality to healthcare, there's a host of businesses that can benefit from your service.

11.6. Financial Sustainability

The financial side of sustainability means your business needs to bring in more money than it's spending. You can do this by negotiating better rates with your clients, controlling overhead costs, and ensuring you pay your shoppers fairly but sustainably. Regular financial audits can help keep track and manage your cash flow effectively.

11.7. Implementing Sustainable Practices

Lastly, sustainability means looking beyond finances. Integrate environmental and social sustainability into your business practices. This could be as simple as going paperless or encouraging your shoppers to use public transport for assignments.

All in all, growth and sustainability are dual objectives that require balance. Growth should be pursued so long as it does not endanger sustainability, while sustainability should not stifle growth. Navigating this can be an art in itself. But, with careful planning, patience, and adaptability, your mystery shopping empire can not only thrive but also become an industry powerhouse that inspires respect and awe.

www.ingramcontent.com/pod-product-compliance
Lightning Source LLC
Chambersburg PA
CBHW060859260726
48661CB00008B/3343